PRACTICING SELF-LOVE

Choosing Happiness Through Conscious Decisions and Accepting Yourself

Sharon Gloria Jenkins

DISCLAIMER:

The advice provided in this material is general only. It has been prepared without taking into account your objectives, financial situation, or needs. Before acting on this advice you should consider the appropriateness of the advice, having regard to your objectives, financial situation, and needs. Where quoted, past performance is not indicative of future performance. The author and the publisher of this book disclaim all and any guarantees, undertakings warranties, expressed or implied, and shall not be liable for any loss or damage whatsoever (including human or computer error, negligent or otherwise, or incidental or consequential loss or damage) arising out of or in connection with any use or reliance on the information or advice on this site. The user must accept sole responsibility associated with the use of this material, irrespective of the purpose for which such use or results are applied. The information in this material is no substitute for financial advice.

Table of contents:

Introduction/Overview

It was Abraham Lincoln, who said that one can only be as happy as one chooses to be. Undoubtedly, this proverb carries a lot of weight and meaning, which can be explained by the fact that happiness begins with a choice. So, if you decide to be happy, the question is: what should you choose to be happy? While there are many things you could consider to be happy, accepting yourself for who you are should be the foundation of your happiness. That is, you choose to be happy by accepting yourself.

Many of us believe that we don't need happiness to be defined for us because we can identify it when we see it or feel it. Happiness is used to describe many positive emotions, such as contentment, joy, gratitude, pride, etc.

Undoubtedly, happiness is a universal phenomenon that we all long to experience more of, but more often than not we find ourselves moody, angry, depressed, etc. But through self-acceptance, happiness can be your norm. When you accept yourself for who you are, you will love yourself more and more every day, you will not live your life in scarcity, you will be grateful for everything you have, you will not even compare yourself to others, the right person will be attracted to you, you will meet and connect with more people like you, you will be comfortable with the stage of life you are in, you will not consider yourself a failure, you will be much more aware of your surroundings and you will have more opportunities.

Life is meant to be enjoyed. Don't allow yourself to be miserable. While there are times when you will feel disappointed, sad, lonely, etc., don't allow that feeling to consume you. Accepting yourself means not allowing any factor inside or outside of you to define your happiness.

Being happy makes you glow. It makes you feel good about yourself. Happiness gives you a springy step, makes you walk with confidence and also makes you radiate positive energy wherever you go. Everyone will prefer such a feeling to going into the dark room of sadness.

Your working hours will fly by when you are happy because the happiness energy will be diverted to your task and you will enjoy the work. As a result, you perform your work efficiently and complete your task faster.

When you are not preoccupied with sad thoughts or worries, your creative juices flow freely.

This book was therefore written to show you ways to learn to accept yourself and what other means you can use to make yourself happy and live a more fulfilling life. The world needs happier people to make it a better place for you and me. Making the effort necessary to become happy is a worthwhile investment. Make the decision today to be happy.

Simple Actions That Can Transform Your Life

Have you noticed that there are people who will always be happy irrespective of whatever happens to them? Do you also see how they always maintain a positive perspective about life? Has it even come to your notice that these people enjoy things more than both you and I could imagine? Not to forget, do you also see that they have thriving relationships in both their professional and personal life? Is there any trick or magic that makes their lives enviable? Well, no. There is no special guide to their happiness other than what you already know. It's just that you don't recognize them as a tool you need to live a happier life. Or you just don't put them into practice. So, how do you go about it? Simple. All you have to do is just to inculcate these actions that will be discussed below, and see your life moving from being happy to becoming happier.

These habits should be practiced in your daily routine, and let's see if you won't experience something life-changing.

1. Breathing and posture

Interestingly, breathing and posture are some of the most natural ways of putting yourself on the path of happiness. However, the importance of breathing is so underrated that we don't even consider it a vehicle for happiness.

So how do you go about breathing and making effective postures? The first thing is to sit straight, and pushing your shoulders backward, then proceed to take a deep breath. Try this a few more times, how do you feel?

Your focus should be taking a deep breath as many times as possible while sitting up with your shoulder back.

2. Join an initiative you are passionate about

You can volunteer your time with an NGO. One of the simplest ways of becoming happy is helping people, particularly those that are in need. Check your neighborhood, or online for something you are passionate about, then lend your helping hands. Mind you, helping someone can be addictive, not only because you are sparing your time to help people, but because it makes you feel good, and the good feeling can be addictive. On the other hand, helping people is one of the ways you can be appreciative of the blessings you have received, as well as a humbling way of contributing to humanity.

There are scores of reasons why you will be happy if you engage in volunteering your time for a course you believe in. Try it today, and feel unmatched happiness.

3. Challenge yourself

Another way you can make yourself happy is by setting a goal and achieving it. The happiness will come from finding a solution to the challenges you encounter on the path to your goal, while the bigger happiness comes from achieving your goal.

Also, in addition to getting happiness from solving a problem, you will get to improve yourself, which often time leads to double happiness with both your accomplishment and your goal.

To make this task interesting for yourself, you can start with small goals, and ensure that you celebrate the small success, then move to a bigger one. Setting and achieving small goals increase your confidence, and equally, make you feel happy and good about yourself.

4. Be comfortable with your negativity

A lot of people try as much as possible to distance themselves from what they find negative about themselves. Some even think that repressing these feelings will make them happy, but the reverse is the case, it will only make them sadder, and backfire into stress, physical pains, or even something worse.

The truth is those negative things happen, and you have to be comfortable with them. Sometimes, there are times when things go out of our control, which can potentially make you stressed.

If you learn to accept that there is nothing you can do about the negative things that have happened, you won't feel the emotion to repress it, thereby freeing you to immediately swing back to things that make you happy.

5. Exercise often

The importance of exercise in relation to happiness has been scientifically explored, and studies have revealed that regular exercise can make one happy, as it helps with relieving stress, makes one feel good, boost confidence, and so on. The *"feel good"* feeling after exercise is a result of the endorphin that is released in the brain after performing any physical activity. It is also worthy of note, that you don't have to undertake an hour-long rigorous exercise before you feel good. Studies have shown that 30 or 10 minutes of light exercise is as effective as 1 or two hours of exercise. You should, therefore, be able to spare at least 10 minutes for exercise.

6. Smile often

You can make it a habit to exchange a smile with whoever you meet on the road. One of the universal body language everyone understands is smiling. If you smile with people, and they return the smile, it will make you feel good.
You can brighten up the day of people you come in contact with, just with a flash of a smile. You should therefore take smiling as a regular habit. On the other hand, smiling also makes people easily get comfortable with you, and make you approachable.

7. Be comfortable with your fears

Fear feasts on people's happiness. There is no how both fear and happiness can co-exist. Fear is a catalyst of negativity, stress, and worry. If you want to deal with fear, you need to start embracing and being comfortable with it.

Although fear is a natural phenomenon. But whenever you are scared, reaffirm to yourself that you are strong enough to handle whatever situation life presents you. You can start tackling your fears by starting small. As you take it step-by-step, you will notice that you start becoming happier, confident, and stronger with how you tackle your fears.

8. Meditate often

You need to give meditation a real chance if you have been perceiving meditation as a strange or spiritual practice. Meditation has been scientifically confirmed to help facilitate happiness, and enable people to live a happier life.

If you try meditating, you will be exposed to other health benefits of meditation, which will contribute to your overall general health. To start meditating, try to focus on the rhythm of your breath for five to ten minutes per day, and pay attention to whatever feeling you are experiencing at that point in time if it is a negative or positive feeling. If it is negative, be comfortable with it, and understand that you will go by diverting your mind to something more positive. And if it is positive, try as much as possible to enjoy and feel the moment.

9. Be grateful and appreciative

It is rewarding to be grateful and appreciative of what you have. This is why is it important to learn to show appreciation. Studies have revealed that those who show appreciation and are grateful often, have a more positive outlook on life, and are even happier.

There are many things you could be grateful for. Be grateful for being alive to see your loved ones. Be grateful for the food you eat. Be grateful that you are not admitted to the hospital, etc. There are many things you can be grateful for. All you need is just to notice your surroundings, and pick from them. It is just a matter of time before your perspective change about life if you are consistent with this approach.

10. Get a new hobby

It is no news that one of the ways to become happy is through hobbies. You should find something you like, and start learning it. It can be playing a particular game, painting cooking, etc. If you already have a hobby you enjoy, great! Soak yourself in it, and see how happiness will start overflowing in your life.

If you are learning a new hobby, pay attention to the thrill of experiencing something new from what you already know. When in the process of learning, you will find something interesting about being new to the hobby, which will come together to give you an enriching experience.

11. Have a life list

Having a life list is one thing everyone should have. The life list helps to give meaning and direction to our life.

Think about what you would like to achieve before you die. This can be a very inspirational, and life-changing experience, especially if you have started achieving what you have on the list. Even though it seems like an archaic pursuit, it is worth it.

12. Expose yourself to sunlight

It has been scientifically proven that sunlight has the necessary properties to make you happy. The skin generates vitamin D when the UV Rays beam on the skin. You will be vulnerable to depression if you lack vitamin D in your system. A signal is sent to your brain to reduce the secretion of melatonin when the sunlight beams on your eye. Melatonin is the hormone that facilitates sleeping and expedites the secretion of serotonin, which is a hormone responsible for wakefulness and happiness.

In essence, what do all these translate to? It means that you will likely be happier when you open up yourself to sunlight. If you can expose yourself to sunlight for at least 15 minutes per day, it will have a positive reaction to your daily mood. Instead of spending time watching TV, you can go for a walk, sit outside during launch, and so on. The most important thing is for the sun to touch your body.

13. Acquire a new perspective

There are a lot of reasons why you can decide not to be happy in this present world. It can be bad grades, struggling to meet up with your needs, a nagging boss, the death of a loved one, etc. The list is endless.

However, you have to note that when you feel sad, what it means is that you have allowed an external force to take charge of your life. At this point, you are no longer in control. But the interesting thing is that you can gain back control of your feeling by changing your perspective. You will transform your whole world when you learn to change your perspective.

Take, for instance, let's take a scenario. You are coming back from work on a Thursday evening with your car, and someone bashed your car from the back. Instead of getting angry with such a person, you can change your perspective by making excuse for such people, like perhaps, they are in a hurry to meet up with an emergency, thus the reason for their impatience, and hoping that they can get to the house on time, to save whoever is involved. Your excuse will make the wrongdoing not affect you.

You, therefore, need to understand that your perception affects your reality.

Mastering Your Mind

You must know that you are the one in charge of what you think. That is the thinker and observer of what is going on in both your mind and environment. Nature has endowed humans with the ability to control his or her thoughts. You, therefore, have to start paying attention to determine, who or what runs the show, for you to know the technique you will use.

You are advised to start paying attention to your thoughts so that when your thoughts start moving towards a direction you find unpleasant; you can catch yourself.

It is advisable to start each of your days to think about any thought you harbor.

You can control your thoughts using these proposed techniques:

> First technique: Eliminate your thoughts altogether
> Second technique: Interrupt then replace the thought

Many people consider the first option as the foundation of peace of mind.

If you adopt the interruption and replacing technique, it will help you restructure your subconscious mind. As you continue to adopt the strategy, the replacement strategy will be the strategy to *"run to"* in applicable situations.

You can adopt technique a for Worrier and Inner Critics, while another technique will be perfect for Sleep Depriver, and Reactor.

1. The Worrier

It is a well-established fact that the ripple effect of prolonged anxiety causes a big disaster to the physical and mental health, which can have a long-term effect on your health, if not properly managed.

One of the triggers of our fight or flight response is fear. And fear is known to bring about worrying, and eventually develops into anxiety in the body. This is one of the reasons why you can't effectively control your thoughts.

By noting how you feel, you will be able to recognize your *"worry thought."* These are some of the physiological signs to consider when your flight or fight response to fear occurs:

- ➢ Muscles tense
- ➢ Breathlessness or shallow breathing
- ➢ A surge of adrenaline, or increased blood pressure or heart rate

These techniques will help interrupt your thoughts as a worrier, then replace them. You might not easily figure out what to replace your thoughts with, if that is the case, you can substitute it with gratitude.

This is the moment to engage a spiritual being if you believe in a higher power. Consider this example:

I can never be scared when the people I love are traveling in bad weather. I will rather say (say a prayer):

> *"I am grateful for looking after ____________. I am appreciative of the fact that you will prevent his/her car from a road accident, and maintenance-free till he/she arrives at his/her destination. I thank you for already encircling the car with your protective hands. May you be exalted forever."*

You have to visualize what you are praying for, as it will bring about the feeling of fulfillment, which will consequently help to put your mind at rest.

When you are done, slowly breathe in, and release the air through your mouth. Repeat for as many times as possible till you feel you are already in control of whatever thought on your mind.

Your reactionary behavior will reduce if you replace your fearful thoughts with appreciation.

Let's take for example you lost sight of your kid in the park. The normal reaction of every parent will be of course fearful, and eventually, yell at the child when found. The parent is likely to say something like: *"Haven't I told you not to leave my sight?"* On the other hand, from the kid's side, his or her reaction will also be fearful of being lost in the first place. In addition to that, the kid will also be extra-conscious, as he knows his dad and mom will be mad whenever he or she makes a mistake, which can make the kid not telling his or her parent the truth about a situation in the future.

An alternative reaction can be: *"I am grateful (the higher power you believe in) for keeping my child safe. And thank you for making me find him too."*

After that thought process, you then find your child. Of course, your reaction will be gratitude.

2. The Inner Critics

You can preferably interrupt your thought if you catch yourself building up negative thoughts about yourself such as disrespecting, berating, or calling yourself names.

You don't have to be dramatic about how you interrupt your thoughts. A simple ENOUGH! or STOP in your mind will suffice. You can then replace it with the opposite of what is trying to manifest in your mind. You can even make some affirmations to yourself starting with the "I am" sentence.

For instance, your thoughts can be reaffirming that you are a loser, you can replace the thought with: "I approve and love myself the way I am. I am beautiful, brilliant, and magnificent. I am a complete spiritual being learning in the journey of life. I am a divine creation of the universal spirit. And I am me."

If you know whose voice it is, you can also consider talking to yourself to thwart the "voice" that developed the thought.

"For the fact that these people said I don't amount to anything doesn't mean they are right. It is just their opinion. Or perhaps, they are just joking, and I considered it seriously because of my insecurity."

As soon as you notice that your self-critic refuses to fade into the background, it is advisable to pen down a reaffirmation or a counter-thought, for you to neutralize how it makes you feel

Necessarily or forcefully, you need to do away with these squatters:

> They try to make you believe that you are not worth anything, as they destroy your self-esteem.
> They are emotionally and verbally abusive.
> You will find then when you try to fall asleep, so they cause the Sleep Depriver.
> They rile up the Worrier
> The name you have been calling yourself manifests into a trigger when others call you by those names.

Get them out of your head. They are all liars!

You will be energized to kill the three squatters if you do jettison your worst critic.

You can begin to replace them with your loved ones who enhance your life, encourage and support you. That is what should dominate your mind.

3. The Sleep Depriver

This variant is the combination of the Worrier and the Inner Critic along with the Ruminator, and the Rehasher, and Planner)

Here is a strategy on how to eliminate the Sleep Depriver and its associates, and master your mind:

> Focus on the rise and fall of your belly, as you pay attention to your deep breath, but that only staves off the thoughts for a short time.

> Afterward, you can figure out a replacement technique that will help keep you off the uncontrolled thoughts dominating your mind. While breathing "in", imagine the word, and the same thing for "out" while breathing out. The words can be stretched for as long as the breath lasts.

You can try it, and see how effective it is. When you catch yourself thinking, quickly adopt the breathing technique. Although that doesn't shut it off, you will put yourself in control. You will be in charge of your thoughts and mind, and you can choose quietly.

Most times, what will further happen when you practice this technique is to start yawning after a few circles, and after few minutes, you fall asleep.

Proceed with this technique if you always find it difficult to sleep at night as a result of your unquiet mind.

You can use this technique any time of the day you wish to. Here is to go about it:

> If you wake up too soon, just fall back asleep
> Try to pause your thinking for a while
> Calm yourself
> Then pay attention to the present moment

4. The Reactor, Troublemaker, or Over-Reactor

More of your attention would be required if you want to eliminate squatters permanently. And you may have to reflect to identify the root cause of your triggers. However, till then, you can still debar the reactor from going overboard as soon as you recognize its presence by starting conscious breathing.

Similar to the Worrier, the feelings or thoughts of the reactor instigates the flight or fight response. The physiological signs are usually the same. You will of course be able to distinguish between anger, anxiety, and frustration if you will pay a little more attention.

You can count 1-10 when you are in a state of anger. But it can be better when you are breathing consciously for that moment. It is very simple, just as how it sounds. All that is required of you is just to be conscious while breathing. Focus on how the air enters through your nose, and how it is released.

5. As you breathe in through your nose:

- ➢ Pay attention to the air passing through your nose.
- ➢ Feel the lungs expanding
- ➢ Pay attention to the rising of your belly

6. Breathing out through your nose:

- ➢ Feel the emptiness of your lungs
- ➢ Pay attention to the falling of your belly
- ➢ Pay attention to the air leaving your nostril.

You can do this as many times as you want. If necessary, just walk away from the situation. This will push in the adrenaline that will enable you to go back to your default settings. Thereby, making you see and address the situation in a logical, and calmer perspective, when you are already in charge of your thought, without it damaging your behavior.

Adding to the problems of the Sleep Depriver is one of the troubles the squatter causes. You will decrease reactionary behavior when you have grown the ability to control or evict the Reactor, which can reduce the need to ruminate and rehash the need to prevent you from falling asleep.

You, therefore, have to develop the ability to master your mind and prevent the Reaction from inviting stress into your life, and relationships.

7. The bottom line

You need to understand that your mind can do so many things you can't even imagine. It can be used for both destructive and constructive purposes. It is up to you fully engage the power it carries.

You have the choice to choose joy, peace, love, gratitude, and compassion, or choose destructive, and undesirable thoughts.

Exercise control over your mind today. Your mind can be what you rely on to encourage you when you feel down. Your mind can be your biggest support, and your best friend. You can the power. Use it.

How to Accept Yourself and Be Happy

1. Consider yourself as a work in progress
2. Practice mindfulness
3. Separate yourself from your performance
4. Try your best knowing that you have done all you could
5. Avoid worrying
6. Pay no attention to what people think about you
7. Use positive talks
8. Be comfortable with your imperfections
9. Deliberately prevent negative thinking pattern
10. Concentrate on your positive thinking

The Reasons You Should Be Happy Now

1. Happy people are healthier

By eating right, and exercising regularly, happy people take care of themselves compared to unhappy people. It means if you love yourself, you will take care of yourself. What are you waiting for? You deserve to be happy. Why not choose happiness now!

It was Marcus Aurelius that said the quality of one's life, is determined by the quality of one's thought, and he encouraged people to watch their thoughts, and ensure that they don't entertain unsuitable thoughts in their mind.

2. Happy people enjoy a better relationship

Many studies have revealed that the average married couple is happier than those that are single. This doesn't necessarily mean you have to be married to be happy. It means you are likely to have a healthier and happy professional and personal relationship with your family and friends when you decide to be happy.

3. That you are alive

Irrespective of whatever has happened to you. There is always one thing you can be grateful for. And one of such include the fact that you are alive. People die regularly, but you are still alive. Be happy, and enjoy every moment it presents to you. When there is life, there is hope. Life is a beautiful thing. Live like today is your last day on earth. Would you spend your life thinking about what you don't have if today were your last day on earth? No. You will only focus on maximizing the little time you have left by relaxing, laughing, and spending time with your loved ones.

4. Happy people are needed in the world

Omar Khayyam said, this moment is our life, and we should be happy for this moment.
If you check around, you will see that many things are happening that make us usually question the coexistence of humans. There is destruction, poverty, pandemic, famine, and war in the world. Fortunately, good always overcome evil. A ripple effect can be generated from someone happy to the rest of the world. A sad person can't radiate a good vibe, only a happy person can. Choose happiness, and be the change you will like to see.

5. Happy people are productive

Consider someone who is always optimistic, and happy, compared to someone who is always venting and complaining about how life has been unfair, who do you think will accomplish more goals and be more productive? Of course, the happy person. So this is another reason why you should be productive.

6. Anything could happen anytime

Life is so unpredictable, and anything could happen anytime. You could wake up to discover that you have a life-threatening disease, you could lose your job, you could lose a loved one. So, you don't have to wait till tomorrow to be happy. Be happy now, and enjoy every single moment and thrill that comes with it.

7. There are People in Your Life Who Love and Depend on You

Chances are that you will do anything for the most important people in your life. If you are looking for a reason to be happy, this is one of the reasons you should and a place to start from. No matter how bad things are, there is always a person, who loves you unconditionally. Of course, your loved ones won't want to see you unhappy and miserable. So it is a good idea to choose happiness for people who love you. It is what makes your relationships more enjoyable.

8. Some people in your life depend on you and love you

The chances are high that you will do anything within your capacity for your loved ones. In fact, this is one of the strongest reasons to be happy. It is also a good place to start your happiness journey. There are still people who love and care for you no matter how bad things become. Those who love you won't want to see you miserable and sad. You, therefore, have to choose happiness for the sake of your loved ones at least, and that is what makes your relationship interesting.

Simple Actions Capable of Transforming Your Life

It is a fact that change is the only constant thing in life. Consider the condition of the world a few years ago, compared to today. Who would have foreseen that something like Corona Virus would come to play, and prevent us from enjoying our "normal" lives? All trips canceled, shops, schools, and offices closed. Who would have imagined that?

We can't resist change as it is unavoidable. Life will become tougher if you keep trying to resist change. Change is everything that surrounds us and makes the biggest difference in our lives. Change is one of life's nature that will catch up with you, irrespective of the place you are. Therefore, there is no point in trying to avoid it. The only thing you can do is just to adjust to the change and change your life.

Change can come into our lives as a result of crises, the choices we made, and pure chance. And in whatever situation we find ourselves in, we are going to make a choice. What differentiates us is if make the make yourself, or you are constrained to.

Unexpected events (crisis) can't be avoided, because randomness is what challenges our complacency. The only thing within our circle of control is our reaction to these unexpected challenges. Therefore, we can activate positive choices in our lives, through our power to choose.

You will have the opportunity to change your life forever if you utilize the power of choice you have. You will be happier and fulfilled if you create more opportunities to create change in your life.

The most important question at this moment now is: how can you then change your life for the better? These are few things you could do:

1. Find a meaning to your life

You need to set your priorities right in life, and the reasons they are important to you. You need to know what makes you happy, what your dreams are, and how you want to achieve them, and if any other thing is important to you in life.

When you have meaning in life, you will be fixed on a definite direction, and how you want to live your life. Without finding any meaning in your life, you will spend the rest of your life unfocused, and with no definite goal.

2. Have a dream board

It is easy to notice that children love day-dreaming. They are very good at dreaming and visualizing what they would like to become as an adult. They don't only dream, they are filled with beliefs and energy that nothing can stop them from achieving that goal.

But things began to take a new turn as adults. We lost the energy and zeal to dream, and gradually the dreams shrunk, then feel like it is impossible to achieve the dream.

Therefore, for you to have a specific direction, it is advisable to create a dream board. You will acquire the energy and passion to follow your dreams when you see your dreams on a board every day. This will make you start believing the possibility of achieving your dreams.

3. Be determined to achieve your dreams

Achieving your goals means you will have to set a short, medium, and long-term goal, once you are to figure out what your dream looks like, and your priorities in life. So, for your dreams to come through, you need to act on them.
Also, note that your dreams can change. This means that you need to be very flexible with setting and executing your goals. As earlier mentioned, change is the only constant thing in life, and your life needs to reflect that change. Take it step-by-step. Set a small goal, and as you achieve it, reward yourself for it. You will gain the confidence to proceed with bigger goals.

4. Don't hold onto your regret

There is nothing beneficial in holding on to regret. Regret is something that has happened that you can't change. You will miss out on the present and future opportunities, if you keep holding on to regret.

Let it go. There is nothing you can do about it again. You only have control over the present and the future. Therefore, you live your life, now, and how you plan for the future is what will determine how your future will pan out.

You could try the balloon exercise. It is very simple. All you need to do is to get some balloons, blow them to whatever size applicable. Write regret on each of the balloons, and let them go, and float into the air. Say goodbye to your regrets forever as the balloons rise into the air.

This exercise looks simple, but it is very powerful and capable of changing your life forever.

5. Try your mind on really scary things

Trying out new things is about leaving your comfort zone, and testing your limits, and experiencing yourself in a new situation.

For instance, if you are scared of speaking publicly, you can sign up for a public speaking course, fine-tune the skill, then try to speak to a large audience when you have the opportunity to. In addition to such an experience being thrilling, it will also be an avenue for you to learn new things about yourself.

Your first experience as a public speaker might be terrible, but I can assure you that you will feel and perform better afterward. If you continue with the art of speaking publicly, you might end up being a motivational speaker. It is an exciting experience that you will love.

If you want to try out something else you are scared of doing, have a plan on how you will execute them. Continue going out of your comfort zone, there are lessons and growth to acquire by so doing. Most importantly, you will feel happy and more confident after completing the tasks.

6. Live a well-balanced life

As we age, our spiritual, physical, and emotional health deteriorate. Your health condition can't remain at the same forever. The only control you have over your health is to feed your body and mind with appropriate substances.

You will notice some physical changes in your life and will be easier for you to build resilience if you live a well-balanced life. You, therefore, need to place a priority on exercising, as it has a direct impact on both your body and mind.

Eat right, drink a lot of water, and exercising will make you happier, fulfilled, and satisfied.

7. Don't run away from your fears

You can't just decide to ignore your fear and hoping that it will fade away. But the truth is that it won't.

Your fears shouldn't be what will control you. It shouldn't if you would like to change your life for the better. Fears are merely fictitious thoughts dominating the mind, that we have come to believe over time as true.

Fear is a restriction that prevents people from maximizing their potentials and living to the fullest. When your fear is controlling your life, you will feel unfulfilled, discontent, and dissatisfied.

So, if you can face your fear, it means you have taken off the grip fear has on you, which invariably means you are on the path to changing your life for the better.

8. Be okay with who you are

You have to like and accept yourself for who you are for you to be able to instigate change in your life because you are the only one who can create change in your life.

Of course, a time will come when you will feel unwanted or rejected. In fact, there will be people that don't like you. It is therefore your responsibility to love and accept yourself for who you are for you to be able to move forward in life.

You will feel unhappy and discontent if you put yourself down, and wishing that you could have done more.

Don't bother about what people will think. Just live your life Find the courage to love yourself. You don't have to think or be conscious of what people will think. Act on it, if it feels right in your mind, and you will be on your way to creating a life you want.

9. Live in the present

The strong desire to be happy elicits the motivation to change your life. This has made us fixated on the pursuit of happiness, that we even forgot to live in the present moment.

Our pursuit of happiness is not a present state; it is a desire for the future. The attention will give to that future state usually consume us that we miss the opportunity the present presents, and make us disconnected.

If you want to experience happiness at the moment, start by showing gratitude, and appreciating daily. You may also consider having a cup of coffee with your partner or loved ones, you can also join a course you are passionate about, an NGO for instance. These are some of the ways of experiencing happiness at the moment

Don't allow the business of your schedule to distract you from living in the moment, because the moment is all you have. The future is not guaranteed.

10. Find joy in learning

You will always gain new knowledge when you learn something new. Learning something new makes you more confident and informed. With learning, you can learn to be more flexible and adapt to new situations or circumstances. Learning allows us to be innovative and creative in our approach to solving a problem, and also in the way we think, hence making us be at peace with the unknown.

Inculcating a reading habit is one of the best ways of learning new things. Life is worthwhile with continuous learning.

Now the choice is yours to change your life. Acting on these tips will not only make you happy but will also change your life for the better.

Don't wait any longer. Act now!

The Importance of Focusing on the Present Moment

Living in the moment has been mentioned in the previous chapter, and you might probably wonder what it means or how it performed. This section of the book is written to put you through all you need to know about living in the present or moment.

In the course of our life journey, we have probably heard something like:

> ➢ *"Live in the moment. Avoid being trapped in the past or the future"*

> ➢ *Be active and present in your own life."*

> ➢ *"All you have is right now. Avoid letting it slip away."*

> ➢ *"All you have is the moment. Don't let it slip away."*

These statements mean the same thing. That is, you shouldn't wallow in the past, or get caught up in the anxiety that will make you worried about the future, and that you should live for now.

In this twenty-first century, it is not easy to live in the moment because something will always come up that will require one to anticipate or prepare. Besides, it is easier to get lost in the past, because of how our past is so well documented, personally or generally. Also, bad events or experiences that cause regret contributes to the reason why some people get lost in the past.

As a result of the jam-packed schedule will have, it is now a norm for anxiety, unhappiness, and stress to be the order of the day. That alone is capable of making us stuck in the past or future, without even realizing it, making one feels worn out.

A lot of research has been conducted on finding a solution to this situation, and the outcome of the research has been consistent with results such as commitment to staying in the moment, and conscious awareness. It is also worthy of note that the solution to a lot of problems is staying in the now.

Staying in the moment might sound great to the ear, but we need to ask ourselves what exactly it means to stay in the present? Is there any other way we could live rather than the moment? This is what this section of the book is focused on answering. Continue reading to discover more.

Before we move further, it is important to clarify that living in the moment is a scientifically and evidenced-backed lifestyle, which is usually recommended by therapists for people struggling with their daily life, anxiety, depression, etc. It is not just an arbitrary term or a popular phrase.

The Meaning of Living in the Present Moment?

Living in the present moment simply means being aware and mindful of what is happening in and around you right now. It is also the state of mind, where you are not stuck or distracted by either in the past or future. You are in the middle, which is the present moment. According to Thum, 2008, if you want to live in the now, a hundred percent of your attention must be diverted to the present.

Myrko Thum further explained that: whatever will happen and will ever happen can only occur in the present moment. Everything that happens, occurred in the present moment. The present moment is the only point we can access time. It is the point between the past and future. It is the only thing where there is no time, and nothing can exist outside it.

Why is Important to be Present Minded?

You want to stay healthy and happy? Then stay in the present moment, as it is the key to it. Living in the present allows you to fight anxiety, rumination, and worry. It is also what keeps you connected to everything around you, and yourself.

Even though over the years, being in the present moment has become a popular and trendy topic everywhere you go, you have to note that it is not a crack to an effective lifestyle or a fad, it is scientifically backed.

According to Halliwell, 2017, living in the present can improve our ability to cope with negative feelings such as anger, and fear, reduce and decrease the impact of stress on the health, can be effective in treating pain, and increasing our ability to be happier and mindful.

Why It Is Difficult to Live in the Present Moment

It is obvious why it is not easy to live in the present moment. We have always been regaled with the idea of thinking about our past or future since we began to have a grasp of our human society operates. Everything around us keeps pushing the past or the future down our throat, ranging from alerts, reminders, advertisements, notifications, etc.

Have you ever thought about how your mobile devices help to keep you in the present moment? Can you remember the last time you were so engrossed in an activity, and your phone suddenly beeped? Do you now notice how much of a distraction it constitutes?

It is no doubt that the mobile phone is one of the best breakthroughs of technology, which can do a lot than imagined. However, this piece of technology has found its way of dominating our daily life, thus distracting us from reality, which is why we need to take a break from it once in a while.

Here are other reasons why it is difficult to live in the present moment:

1. Most times, we try as much as possible to erase the bad part of our experience, which makes it appear like we have a better past than what is coming in the future.
2. Living in the moment can elicit a lot of uncertainties, which is why we get anxious about what is to come.
3. It is natural for the mind to sometimes wander.

While it is not easy to combat these factors, they are not impossible to combat, because we have control over ourselves. We have the power to decide what we want, and how to overcome harmful, or destructive urges.

Finding a balance between the Past, Present, and Future

We can't sometimes avoid thinking about the past or the future.

There is no how we would make progress if we aren't thinking about how to learn from our past mistakes to achieve success. We won't even be anywhere if we don't plan for the future or get ready for what is coming ahead. So being in the moment doesn't mean all these won't happen. It is about not allowing the past or the future to debar you from happiness or making progress.

You can't have a happy or healthy life if you don't spend some time thinking about what happened in the past or the future. What we do most times is to intently focus on this past or the future, which drains us some positive energy.

It is therefore essential for you to be able to balance your thought of the past, present, and future if you want to have a healthy mental condition. It will have a negative effect on your life if you spend time thinking too much about any of these three. Hence the need to strike a balance between the three for a healthy and happy lifestyle.

Although you might not know what the right balance is, when you have attained it, you will experience the majority of your life in the present with less worry, less stress, less anxiety, and so on.

How You can be in Present and Live in the Moment

To attain balance in the past and present, you may consider these tips:

> - If it is not necessary, don't think about the past. When thinking about the past, ensure it is only for important reasons. For example, you can only think about the past when you are trying to find out what made you succeed in your last endeavor when you want to relieve your past stress, or you want to see where you went wrong.

- ➤ The future should only be thought about in small doses, and only pay attention to it, in a low-anxiety and healthy way. For example, if you want to think about the future, only focus on it as required while preparing for it, then move on from there.

- ➤ For the majority of your time, always remain in the present.

You will get better at it when you practice because this guideline is not as simple as it looks.

Living in the Present and also Plan for the Future

This might seem delicate to maintain, but it is not impossible. You can learn to effectively balance these complexities.

Spending time on the present moment or mindfulness doesn't mean denying or ignoring the past or future thought. It has to do with not wasting your time to dwell on them such that they begin to affect your mental health. You can welcome both your past and future thoughts, categorize them, and note their importance. But they shouldn't consume you.

According to Andy Puddicombe of Headspace, the most crucial thing is not to get engulfed in the thought of the past or the future. There is a way we can maintain our consciousness in the present state, while also thinking about past events, without being overwhelmed or distracted by them.

Thinking about the past should be solely for the sake of anticipating what is likely to come without feeling anxious or overwhelmed. When you are living in the moment, and conscious, you won't get caught up in your thought about the future, and get stuck in the past

How to Stop Worrying with Present Moment Awareness?

These are five helpful tips that will make you get rid of excessive anxiety, and stay more connected to the present:

1. By letting go and not thinking about your performance, you can practice unselfconsciousness.

2. Savor the moment. You will avoid bothering about the future by fully experiencing the present.

3. Pay attention to your breathing. Be at peace with yourself through your breathing, stay relaxed and calm, and your interaction with others will be smoother.

4. Lose track of your time, as it will enable you to make it most of it, and find your flow.

5. Be accepting. You don't have to run away from a problem, or whatever is bothering you. You should rather embrace it.

How Practicing Forgiveness Will Set You Free

It was Mahatma Gandhi that said: Forgiveness is the attribute of the strong. The weak can never forgive.

Forgiveness is all about making the decision to repeal revengeful words or stop feeling resentful against someone who has offended you.

Forgiving means that you have let go of hatred, hurt, or forgone your retribution, against someone. The reason for this is simple. Your energy is zapped when you radiate negative emotions, which hate is part of. Your body generates negative chemistry when you have negative thoughts about others.

How Forgiveness Affects You?

We are compassionate and have a good heart by nature. Human energy smoothly flows through this nature. However, you will obstruct a natural flow of energy when you radiate negative energies such as criticism of other, judgments, and negative thoughts. This further prevents and disrupts your body from replenishing your positive energy that can bring about illness.

If you forgive, you will have peace of mind. Forgiving means you are releasing the negative energy that you had a firm grip on. When you forgive, you will develop the ability to identify the pains you suffered without making the pain become your reality, which allows you to proceed with your normal life.

Why is it so Hard to Forgive?

One of the most common perceptions about forgiveness is that it stands based on condoning bad behaviors, and indirectly saying that the person who sinned has done something not bad, no matter how bad it may seem. Forgiveness is about allowing yourself to let go of negative energies, and freeing yourself, and does not mean always reconciling, forgetting, or excusing what the person has done to you.

If anyone has offended you, get in touch with the person right now, tell him or her what he or she did without holding back, then forgive them. By so doing you have released yourself of the negative energy you carry.

Happiness Routine for 1-month

Week 1: Develop a happiness routine

Show gratitude: The connection between gratitude and happiness is very strong. You will be able to deal with adversity, improve your health, and feel more positive emotions if you always express gratitude.

Listen to music: You can feel uplifted by listening to music-- especially if it is your favorite music. Dopamine, which is a feel-good chemical will be released in your brain when listening to music, and that will in turn make you feel good.

Self-love: You will become happier if you love yourself. You may not be able to love someone else properly if you don't love yourself first, because the same psychology applies to both. Check it, you will do anything to make the person you love happier. Also, on the other hand, if you love yourself, you will do anything to make yourself happy.

Physiology: You will develop some physiological changes when you are happy. You will acquire positive emotions, and be more optimistic.

Anchoring: This is a very effective approach to making yourself happy. With anchoring, you will be able to gain access to the past and connecting it to the future. When you anchor yourself into a positive emotion by focusing on the time you felt loved, happy, confident, and motivated. You will feel some positive emotions when those memories flood back.

Incantation: You will have to say something positive to yourself. It is just like an affirmation. By so doing, you will close down negative thoughts that dominate your mind.

Happiness meditation: You will be creating the environment to experience happiness when you start engaging in happiness meditation. You will be developing necessities for happiness which are inner balance, empathy, and playfulness. You will be able to reconnect with your happy state of mind when these aspects of your daily routine are integrated.

Week 2: develop a happy mind

The Now: According to the psychologist, they propounded that distracted people are mostly unhappy, and that is why it is advisable to live in the moment. You will found happiness by living in the moment. It means you will be engrossed in neither the past nor the future. By living in the moment, you will be able to handle emotions such as anger, sadness, reduce stress, and anxiety. Take some break and pay attention to your current state of mind, and environment.

Happy thoughts: All you have to do is just think about things that make you happy. This technique is very close to anchoring. Your mind will return to the time you are happy if you focus on it.

Perspective: Sometimes, your perspective about a situation can be the only preventing factor of your happiness. Try to note the perspective, with which you use to view situations, and try to see if there is a way you could adjust such perspective in a positive light.

Authenticity: You won't need to impress anyone if you are real to yourself. You don't have to impress anyone at the risk of your happiness. Find peace within yourself and try to be real. Your no should be your no, and never feel bad about it.

Beliefs: A lot of people derive happiness from their religion. Research has revealed that religiosity can help with physical well-being, good mental health, and reduced anxiety. If you practice any religion, renew your interest in it, and find happiness.

Forgiveness: It has been earlier mentioned that forgiveness can make one happy. Additionally, forgiveness has been linked to increased feelings of well-being, reduced anxiety, stress, and depression.

Laughter: Laugh often. You can watch comedy shows, read funny write-ups and have fun generally. When you laugh often, you will release the feel-good hormone in your bloodstreams, such as dopamine, endorphin, and serotonin, which will make you feel uplifted and positive.

Week 3: Develop a happy life for yourself

Participate in joyful activities: there will always be an activity that makes you happy each time you participate in it. It can be sport, dancing, meeting with friends, games, etc. The most important thing is to fix more of the activity into your schedule.

Participate in social activities: being in a position to contribute to a course, or being able to help people can make you happy. You can decide to attend social events or volunteer.

Enjoy nature: Spending time with nature can improve your well-being and mood. Experiencing nature will also help you reduce stress. Hear the birds singing, listen to the roaring to the roaring of the ocean, the sound of the air blowing the tree, etc.

Simplicity: Simplify your life. Simplicity comes without stress. Simplify your choices, your behavior, and how you think

Week 4: Create an impact that will last a lifetime

Establish a boundary: creating a boundary is all about taking responsibility for your actions, and not the responsibility for other people. You won't put yourself under unnecessary pressure or situation, that will keep you on your toes.

Spontaneity: Being spontaneous is a desirable trait. You will be more relaxed, and less stressed when you are spontaneous because regardless of whatever happens to you, you are sure that you will be able to handle it.

Contribution: It is all about doing something that will contribute to your goal, that makes other people happy. That can be making other people happy through donations, engaging in social service, spending time with children, etc. If you make other people happy, you will also be happy because happiness is contagious.

Final Thoughts

It is common for many people to get lost in the darkroom of negative feelings of gloom and doom, forgetting how important happiness is to us and those around us. Surprisingly, many people don't realize how unfair they are being to themselves and those around them, because the world needs more happiness to overshadow all the dark times of the past and shine a more positive light on the future.

Moreover, luck is equally important to help us and many other people to use their latent talents and achieve their ambitions and goals in life.

Happiness is a way of life. It is the conscious effort of how you live your life. It is a sense of being. It goes beyond a big smile on your face. You must note, however, that happiness requires effort, and it is hard work. While it may be practically impossible to be happy all the time because life has a way of throwing lemons at us, it is our responsibility to make lemonade out of such a situation. As mentioned earlier, happiness is a choice. Be at peace with yourself first, accept yourself as you are, and spread love. Thereupon, happiness begins.

www.ingramcontent.com/pod-product-compliance
Lightning Source LLC
Chambersburg PA
CBHW040316240726
48664CB00006B/1510